D1154391

# LESSONS
## LEARNED
### on the
# JOURNEY

# LESSONS LEARNED on the JOURNEY

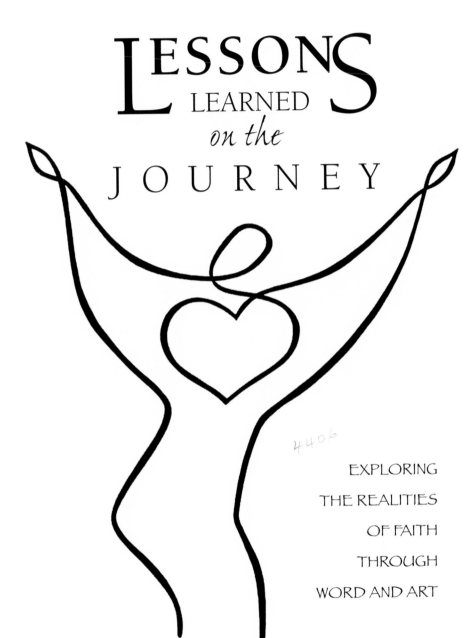

EXPLORING
THE REALITIES
OF FAITH
THROUGH
WORD AND ART

## BOB SNYDER, M.D.
*Illustrated by András Simon*

2 4⁶
SNY
L⁹⁵

Published in the United States by Baxter Press, Friendswood, Texas.
Formatted by Anne McLaughlin, Blue Lake Design, Dickinson, Texas.
Cover design by Chris and Jeannie Leaman, Malvern, Pennsylvania.

ISBN: 1-888237-50-3

The versions of the Bible used in this book are the New International Version and *The Message*. Used by permission.

# Table of Contents

# Preface

*Lessons Learned on the Journey* was conceived in 1996 when our family moved from the suburbs of Philadelphia, Pennsylvania to Budapest, Hungary. I had left 17 years of emergency medicine practice to work with International Health Services – training medical professionals to integrate their faith in Jesus into their medical practices.

During this time of transition my cousin, Dan Wolgemuth, challenged me to begin journaling my thoughts, which ultimately led to this book. The vignettes you will read are from my experiences living and ministering in Central Europe, from practicing medicine, from my marriage and children, and from my growing-up years. Each contains a spiritual lesson.

In preparation, 50 lessons were translated into Hungarian so that my dear friend and Hungarian artist, András Simon, could meditate upon them. András then drew an original print for each lesson. András' desire was

- To create illustrations that, in some cases, would reinforce the thoughts and concepts from a lesson, and in other cases
- To create illustrations that would be the instigator – the seed from which the prose or lesson would grow.

When working with a book from the conception of an idea to a hard backed volume, one realizes that the trip is a group affair. Many walked along side – friends and colleagues, even strangers – with tidbits of advice, editorial change, support and subject matter. The measure of their contribution is impossible to calculate. A part of each person resides within these covers. Thank you.

However, without the diligent editorial labor of my wife, Pamela, and daughter, Emily, this project would never have known completion. Not one line appears that does not bear the mark of their discerning eyes and nuanced edits. I can not thank my wife enough for not only being my editor, but also my partner on the journey. With her the journey has been richer, deeper and fuller.

It is my prayer that you are blessed, perhaps even changed, as you contemplate the words and the art. Thank you for joining me on the journey.

*Bob Snyder, M.D.*

# Gleaning Life's Lessons

As I look back at my college years, I realize that significant lessons were gleaned outside the lecture hall. These life lessons were learned in the dorm room (developing relationships with people very different from myself), on the soccer field (growing in discipline and loyalty) and in the arena of student government (honing leadership skills). Many of my life's best and hardest lessons were learned beyond the four walls of a classroom.

Faith is like that, as well. Most applications of the profound truths of God are not learned in a church or a seminary. Rather, they are encountered:

- In a hospital during the birth of a child or in the death of a loved one.
- In the midst of betrayal or financial crisis.
- At that moment when we are tempted to compromise our faith or our values.

Henri Nouwen, the well-known psychologist and author, exemplified this in his own life. Although he had taught at prestigious universities such as Yale, Harvard and Notre Dame, he learned great spiritual lessons serving the mentally handicapped in L'Arche, an international network of communities. His work with these people enabled him to share deep spiritual truths in his writings that could not have been learned at a university.

Jesus taught his disciples great spiritual truths through sermons and parables, but He gave His disciples ample opportunity to learn through the common tasks of life. In the midst of storms and unsuccessful fishing expeditions, the disciples experienced lessons of faith in tangible and unforgettable ways. We have much to learn in church this week, but many of the great lessons of faith will occur Monday through Saturday. What will God teach us today about faith in the challenges we will encounter?

"I applied my heart to what I observed and learned a lesson from what I saw." (Proverbs 24:32)

# A Life Transformed by Mercy

An act of mercy changed me in high school. Let's open the scene in my high school algebra class. An unannounced quiz caught me by surprise, and I knew little or nothing on the test. In a moment of desperation, I cheated by copying the answers of the person in front of me. Since the answers could be derived by multiple methods, I was easily caught when only two papers in the class were the same – the person's in front of me and mine. That afternoon after school, my algebra teacher pulled me aside from playing in an extracurricular sport. He indicated that he knew I had cheated and that he had the right to flunk me for the whole semester and to tell my parents. Instead, he said that he would only flunk me for that particular exam and would not tell my parents. He continued by saying that he expected me to learn from this experience and to never cheat again. He said that he had confidence in me in spite of what I had done and looked forward to what was ahead for me. Never again did I cheat; because, when tempted, I remembered the mercy shown by my algebra teacher. It left me with a profound understanding of how mercy, shown with great love and expectation, can encourage people to change.

Jesus illustrates this undeserved forgiveness in a parable about mercy. He tells us of a servant who owes the king a great deal of money. As a result of the servant's pleas, the king forgives the entire debt. However, the mercy shown by the king has little impact on the heart of this servant. For, after being relieved of this great debt, the servant demands payment of a small debt that another man owes him. When the debtor is unable to pay, the servant has him thrown into prison. (Matthew 18:21–35). This is an unfortunate example of someone who was not transformed through an encounter with mercy.

Mercy shown in love and with great expectation can be life transforming. It is the essence of the Father's forgiveness through Christ Jesus. What is our response to this gift of mercy? Is there someone in your life who needs the love of Jesus shown through you by an act of mercy?

# Our Feelings or God's Character

I am a moody man – always have been. This is advantageous when my mood is upbeat and I feel encouraged. But when I am pessimistic and discouraged, the effect is less pleasant. Medically, we see the important role our emotional life plays in our physical well-being. Intense emotional experiences affect our blood pressure, pulse and breathing patterns. Loneliness is proven to have a dramatic negative impact on our health. Laughter, on the other hand, is recognized for its health benefits. Our emotions touch every area of our lives – our relationships, our self-esteem, our work and even our spiritual lives.

However, our emotions are often a poor barometer of what is real in life. When my relationship with my wife Pamela is based on my feelings, there is an undulating quality that depends on which wave I am riding – up or down. I am so grateful that our marriage is based, not on feelings, but on our commitment before God and to each other. This provides the solid anchor that keeps us secure in the midst of the storms.

When it comes to my relationship to God, I often depend too much upon my feelings to determine the strength of my connectedness to Him. How dangerous! Our bond with God is not determined by our emotions but on His unchanging attributes and promises.

In commenting on his sense of spiritual dryness, a friend sent me these wise words:

> "Nothing about my relationship with God changes day to day, at least from His point of view. He still loves me the same as always, He still forgives me and assures me of His love and of eternal life. He still is ready to feed me from His bread and to quench my thirst from His fountain. And He does these things whether I have a feeling that matches His actions and attitudes or not!"

Isn't it comforting to know that our relationship with God is not dependent on our fluctuating feelings, but rather on His unwavering character and constant faithfulness? He declares, "I, the Lord, do not change."(Malachi 3:6) Neither will His love for us falter. For he says, "I have loved you with an everlasting love." (Jeremiah 31:3)

Whether we feel like it or not, God's promises remain true, and we may confidently rest in the promises of His unchanging character.

# *Recognizing the Genuine*

I went to medical school eager to practice medicine. My excitement temporarily waned as I took my first course, anatomy and physiology, which focused on the normal characteristics and functions of a healthy human body. When would we get to the study of pathology and disease? The reason for this foundational course soon became evident, for without an understanding of the body's normal anatomy and function, the abnormal could not be detected.

A similar method is used to teach people to identify counterfeit money. Before they can discover a fake, they must have complete knowledge of the genuine. During training people are given money to carry with them. They are encouraged to examine the bills in detail – smell them, feel them and generally become so familiar with the real thing that they can easily detect an imitation.

We need this training spiritually as well. When we do not know the authentic, we are easily susceptible to the counterfeit. As followers of Christ, we find authenticity in Jesus Himself and His words. If we do not know Him well and study his teachings, we can be easily led astray.

In the book of Hebrews we are encouraged to know the authenticity of Jesus. "Remember your leaders, who spoke the word of God to you. Consider the outcome of their way of life and imitate their faith. Jesus Christ is the same yesterday and today and forever. Do not be carried away by all kinds of strange teachings." (Hebrews 13: 7-9a)

Let us be so familiar with the authenticity of Jesus and His Word that the counterfeit will be obvious.

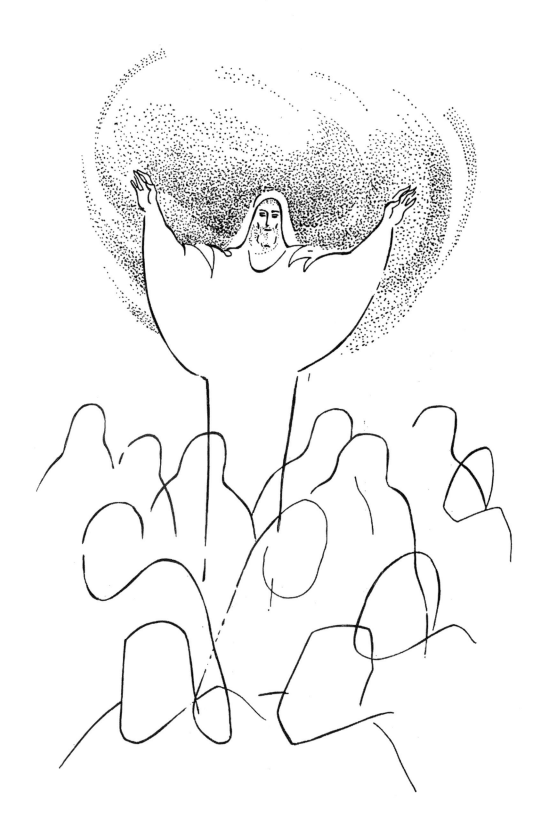

# 5

## Heeding the Correct Message

They were a couple, obviously tourists, pulling suitcases behind them and standing at a complicated and busy intersection. The traffic signal indicated, "Don't Walk." Suddenly, without warning, the woman stepped out into traffic. Cars screeched to a stop, horns blared, and she yelled at the drivers who had "wronged her." It was quite a scene! As the woman continued to scream and point to the walk signal, her husband, clearly embarrassed, pulled her back to the curb. Though he pointed out that she had been looking at the wrong walk signal, the woman remained unrepentant and unfazed. As they walked off, I wondered how often I am like that woman, responding correctly to the wrong message.

We are bombarded by messages every day. Often with good intentions and much sincerity, we respond to incomplete or false messages. These are sometimes direct and other times subtle. And although messages permeate our lives, not all of them are true.

Incomplete or false messages are sometimes communicated:

- By the advertising world when the truth is shaded to encourage us to buy a product.
- By friends and peers who suggest that personal appearance is more important than character.
- By the values of the world that imply that material success, position or power is more important than inner peace.
- By a church that encourages outward piety and forgets the importance of the state of the heart.

As we step out into the busy crosswalk of life and encounter messages, we need to ask the question, "Am I responding to the correct message?" Jesus' message to His disciples and to us today is correct, simple and clear. He said, "Follow me." (John 21:19b)

# Toiling in Obscurity

An old college friend once said to me, "You have an easy life now that you are a doctor." I thought of the long hours at the hospital and the life and death decisions in the emergency department and wondered, "What is so easy?" I thought of medical school – the hours of studying on Friday nights while others were partying. I thought of the moments at 3:00 AM in the hospital as a resident physician. My friend had no idea of the investment of private time and energy required to become a physician.

Hank Hanegraaff's book, *The Prayer of Jesus,* comments on investing wisely in our private lives. Admiring the golf game of Tiger Woods and recognizing the source of his success, Hanegraaff says, "Tiger Woods performs in public the way he practices in private." We often forget the unseen investment as we admire the accomplishments of others.

Jesus recognized the importance of the disciplines of private life when he taught the disciples about prayer. Prior to teaching them what we call, "The Lord's Prayer", Jesus said, "And when you pray, do not be like the hypocrites, for they love to pray standing in the synagogues and on the street corners to be seen by men. I tell you the truth, they have received their reward in full. But when you pray, go into your room, close the door and pray to your Father, who is unseen." (Matthew 6:5-6a)

Jesus must have known that our human nature avoids diligent toil in obscurity. The unseen "roots" of private labor, make sturdy, productive public "stalks" above ground. Without the deep cultivation of a meaningful, disciplined life with Jesus, our public life is often filled with selfish shallowness.

A neurosurgeon friend in training spent countless hours suturing torn tissues together at the bottom of a small cup while looking through a microscope. He did this so that someday a person in great need would receive the benefits of his skill honed during many hours of secret practice.

Are we willing to invest in the unseen, private disciplines to which God calls us, or do we clamor for recognition? Let us cultivate deep roots in relationship with God so that we may grow into strong visible witnesses for Him.

# Pain —A Vehicle to Empathy

Sensitivity to the feelings of others has never come naturally to me. Binding people's physical wounds has been my professional life. However, recognizing and attending to emotional, social and spiritual wounds have been more difficult. A recent shoulder injury reminded me that one of the best ways to become sensitive to the needs of others is to suffer a similar problem.

My shoulder injury left me unable to dress myself. This embarrassing dilemma caused me to think of my grandfather who experienced similar problems dressing due to the traumatic loss of his left hand. I also thought of a friend who had experienced a stroke. I understood, in a small way, some of the problems they both experienced.

Isaiah, prophesying about the coming of Jesus, indicated that the extent of Jesus' experience with mankind would be deep and complete. He would not merely come to rescue us from our sinful state and return to the comforts of heaven. Rather, He chose to suffer. In that suffering, He identifies with us as we walk through difficulties, pain and suffering on this earth. Isaiah 53:3 says, "He was despised and rejected by men, a man of sorrows and familiar with suffering." The ability to empathize with and extend comfort to others is often related to a shared experience. Paul explains in II Corinthians 1:3b–4 that God is "the Father of compassion and the God of all comfort, who comforts us in all our troubles, so that we can comfort those in any trouble with the comfort we ourselves have received from God."

Could difficult circumstances be beneficial, enabling us to cultivate empathy? Has the experience of suffering and pain caused anger and bitterness, or has it brought an increased identity with Jesus and sensitivity to the needs of others? Let us embody Christ's comforting presence in this suffering world, identifying with individuals in pain and bearing a message of hope.

# 8

## *Called to Stewardship*

A recent conversation with my wife Pamela stimulated my thoughts about ownership. With a renewed understanding of who "owns" our children, she shared with me a new attitude of prayer. As she prays for Emily, Julia and Catherine, she says, "Dear God, be with *your* Emily, *your* Julia and *your* Catherine." She explained that it enables her to seek God's desire for the girls more earnestly, rather than focusing upon her desires for them. It is an issue of perceived ownership.

The Bible repeatedly stresses the perspective of stewardship rather than ownership. It impels us to re-examine the way we treat what God has given us. In Genesis 2:15, the Lord put Adam in the Garden of Eden, asking him to work and care for it. God's design is stewardship; however, man's proclivity is ownership. When we choose ownership over stewardship, the results are often not God's best.

A friend once asked me how I would respond if my stockbroker, entrusted with the stewardship of my money, used my money to buy himself a nicer home and a luxury car. I was confused by his question until he continued by asking if I thought God was displeased by the way people used and controlled His possessions, given only to us for our guardianship. I imagine that He is often not pleased.

Let us carefully assess our hearts' attitudes toward that which God has given to us. Is our attitude one of stewardship or one of ownership? Is our stewardship of God's earthly gifts worthy of His trust?

"So if you have not been trustworthy in handling worldly wealth, who will trust you with true riches?" (Luke 16:11)

# 9

# The Excellence of Child-likeness

Splat! While learning to ski in my mid 20's, I often found myself facedown in the snow, and I regularly evaluated my progress by the number of falls per day. My ski instructor informed me that adult beginners spend too much energy trying to prevent falls and too little time enjoying skiing. He pointed out that I would progress faster if I adopted the attitude of a child. Children simply consider falling a part of skiing.

Compare learning life's lessons to learning to ski; child-like attitudes are beneficial to both. Warren Bennis and Burt Nanus, in *Leaders: the Strategies for Taking Charge*, suggest that successful leaders never outgrow child-like behavior. Such leaders, they say, demonstrate their maturity by retaining positive characteristics of a child such as:

- Enthusiasm for people.
- Spontaneity.
- Imagination.
- Unlimited capacity to learn new behavior.

Child-likeness is an asset on the slopes, on the job, and in the home.

Should it surprise us that Jesus suggests the same? In a reprimand to his disciples who were sending little children away, Jesus said, "I tell you the truth, anyone who will not receive the kingdom of God like a little child will never enter it." (Mark 10:15)

Child-like qualities of faith and trust should be greatly desired and nurtured. How quickly we become cynical realists in adulthood. I trust that we will seek to avail ourselves to the child-likeness that Jesus desires in us.

And let us recognize, as my mother often reminded me, there is a difference between child-like behavior and childish behavior. "When I became a man, I put childish ways behind me." (I Corinthians 13:11b)

# More Laughter — Good Medicine

His whole countenance changed. A wide smile, then laughter, filled his face. I was so surprised; I had not seen him laugh in so long! I told my friend, "You look good in laughter." Laughter, indeed, improves our appearance. It benefits many areas of life. As a physician, I have been especially intrigued with laughter's effect on health.

Laughing 100 times is equal to 15 minutes on an exercise bicycle. It can be an exhausting experience as we use our facial, respiratory, abdominal, back and leg muscles. Our blood pressure lowers; blood flow increases; and oxygen into the blood stream increases. Laughing is jogging for our insides.

The health benefits of laughter are significant. When we laugh:

- We experience an increase in gamma-interferon (disease-fighting proteins) and T-cells (a major part of our immune system).
- We experience an increase in natural killer cells (tumor and virus destroying cells) and B-cells (disease-destroying antibodies).
- We experience an increase in immunoglobulin-A which fights respiratory infections such as the common cold.
- We experience a cathartic for negative emotions such as anger, sadness and fear.

Even the author of Proverbs knew that laughter was good for us as he said, "A cheerful heart is good medicine, but a crushed spirit dries up the bones." (Proverbs 17:22) Laughing is beneficial to our physical health, our relationships and our emotional well-being. We need to laugh more often. Taking ourselves too seriously deprives us of our daily doses of laughter.

Let us begin to practice laughter and find the benefits of a cheerful heart, as did the wife of noble character in Proverbs. "She is clothed with strength and dignity; she can laugh at the days to come." (Proverbs 31:25)

## *Always Available*

My daughter Emily acquired a serious ankle injury while running during the summer. When she informed me in late November that she was still experiencing significant pain, I immediately began to search for a competent sports medicine doctor. Although I wanted her to see a doctor before Christmas, securing an appointment with such short notice was not an easy task. Access to competent, in-demand physicians can be a challenge. Receptionists guard their schedules and insurance companies limit access - not a pleasant feeling in a time of need.

I am afraid that my personal life sometimes mirrors this same inaccessibility. I discovered that a person in our church felt uncomfortable approaching me. He sensed that I was not available, thus discouraging the development of a friendship. Although I long for my life to be an example of loving approachability, that is not always the case.

God, on the other hand, is completely reliable in this respect. You don't have to worry about making an appointment. He has no receptionist guarding His schedule. He is never too busy or distracted. "The Lord is near to all who call on him, to all who call on him in truth." (Psalm 145:18) He promises that He is "our refuge and strength, an ever-present help in trouble." (Psalm 46:1) We have no need to be intimidated or discouraged from engaging Him. We can "approach the throne of grace with confidence..." (Hebrews 4:16)

As followers of Jesus, do our lives reflect His likeness? Let us seek to exhibit approachability, as Jesus so graciously does for us. May we point others to the One who is always available and willing to touch us at our point of need.

## *Fretting*

I like the word 'fret' – to give oneself up to resentful discontent, worry and regret. It paints a picture of a person not only worrying, but also wringing his or her hands and saying, "Woe is me!" Admit it; we have all fretted at one time or another.

The issues that cause us to fret, many times, have not even occurred. We fret more often over the future than the present circumstances. The uncertainty of the future is rich breeding ground for fretting. What will happen to the world in the next year? Will my children be safe from the dangers of life? Will they make the "right" choices? Will we have sufficient resources to pay next month's rent or mortgage? Will I get to the meeting on time in the midst of this traffic jam? Fretting about the future, whether the near future or the far-off future, comes so naturally.

A physician friend in Thessalonikki, Greece reminded me that even though God does not allow us to know the future, He does promise to be there in the future with us. It is the ultimate opportunity to practice the essence of faith – trusting Him in the unseen and the unknown – the opposite of fretting!

God's desire, as we journey through life, is that our hearts deepen in our dependence on Him and in our faith in His provision. Fretting, on the other hand, works against faith. The Apostle Paul said, "Don't fret or worry. Instead of worrying, pray. Let petitions and praises shape your worries into prayers, letting God know your concerns. Before you know it, a sense of God's wholeness, everything coming together for good, will come and settle you down. It's wonderful what happens when Christ displaces worry at the center of your life." (Philippians 4:6–7; *The Message*)

The next time we find ourselves "wringing our hands," let's stop for a moment and shape our worry into a faith-filled prayer.

# Building Up or Tearing Down?

Discernment – that ability to see clearly and to deeply understand. When practicing emergency medicine, discerning the critically ill from those who were "just sick" was vital. I tried to teach resident physicians this important skill. Of all the residents, only one of them could not discern the critically ill from the "just sick." I encouraged him to go into research and not to treat patients.

Discernment can, at times, be inappropriately negative. Recalling my college literature class, my assignments included reading the great classics. My professor seemed less than satisfied if I did not negatively critique the material. The goal of discernment, in this case, did not seem to be a positive attribute, but a negative one.

Spiritually, I often find myself using discernment in the same negative way, to analyze, to critique and to find fault. This critical approach is certainly not what Jesus had in mind for spiritual discernment. Oswald Chambers' classic daily devotional, *My Utmost for His Highest*, gives insight into this area. These are some of his comments.

- "If we are not heedful of the way the Spirit of God works in us, we will become spiritual hypocrites. We see where other folks are failing, and we turn our discernment into the gibe of criticism instead of into intercession on their behalf."
- "Discernment is God's call to intercession, never to fault finding."
- "When we discern that people are not growing spiritually and allow the discernment to turn to criticism, we block our way to God. God never gives us discernment in order that we may criticize but that we may intercede."

This is a particularly hard lesson for me since I am prone to criticism. Will you join me in choosing to use discernment to intercede and build up, rather than to judge and tear down?

"Have mercy upon us, O Lord, have mercy upon us: for we are exceedingly filled with contempt." (Psalm 123:3 KJV)

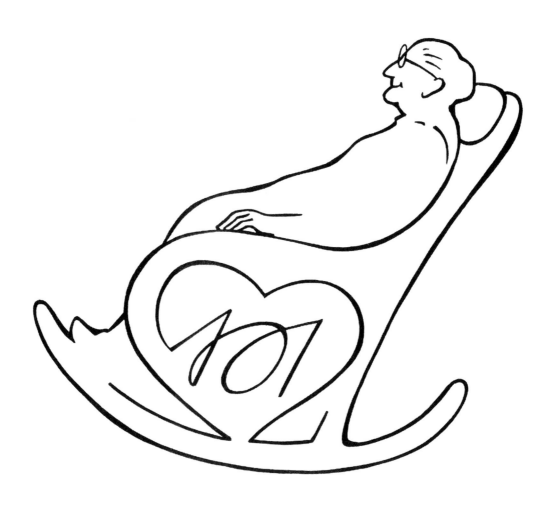

# Aunt Sara

Aunt Sara, my wife's great aunt, is 101 years old, having lived in three different centuries. Amazing! Never married, her life was one of service and simplicity. She has delighted us throughout the years with her contented life.

When Aunt Sara was born in 1899, most people lived in rural locations. The average life expectancy for a woman in the United States was about 48 years. Without antibiotics, infectious diseases were rampant. Cars and airplanes were not a part of daily life. Space travel, computers and ATM machines were the ideas of science fiction writers. She had no idea two world wars, the Korean War, the Vietnam War, the Gulf war, the Iraqi War and countless worldwide conflicts would bring an age of much human suffering and death. In the midst of the world's calamities and the many challenges in her own personal life, Aunt Sara lived contentedly.

In her twilight years, the technological revolution has slipped past her. No, she does not know how to work on a computer. With her modest means, she missed the longest bull stock market in history in the 1990s (and the sudden drop!). How could such contentment and peace resonate from the life of this tiny, frail woman?

Aunt Sara's life was never measured by the amount of material goods she possessed; nor was it gauged by what she had missed in life. Aunt Sara's energy was spent loving God and caring for others. That was enough.

Can loving God and serving others be enough to find contentment in life? At times, we may feel that we cannot be content without a certain job, a certain house or a special car. We may think that contentment is impossible with certain church or political leadership. Perhaps we assume that we could never be content without health or family members.

Contentment comes, not in having what we want in sufficient supply; contentment is an attitude of heart allowing us grateful acceptance of what we possess. "But godliness with contentment is great gain. For we brought nothing into the world, and we take nothing out of it." (I Timothy 6:6–7). Do we really believe that?

Each day brings more change and challenges for each of us. Will loving God and serving others be the basis of our contentment or will we seek it elsewhere? Let's follow Aunt Sara's example.

# Weakness — an Advantage?

"What is your greatest weakness?" This question, posed during one of my interviews for entrance into medical school, caught me off guard. I quickly tried to give an answer that would sound real enough to satisfy the interviewer, but not bad enough to prevent my acceptance into medical school. The result was denial, embarrassment and cover-up.

I did not understand that frailty, disability, powerlessness or failure could have any positive purpose. A pastor-friend from Budapest challenged my thinking. He asked, "If dependency on God is a goal, could weakness be an advantage?" An advantage?

Dependency on God implies that we are in need, meaning that our own abilities, talents, strengths, money or positions are not enough. What a humbling thought! Could weakness be a means by which God enables us to depend on Him?

The apostle Paul, in II Corinthians 12, declared that he could boast and delight in weakness, "so that Christ's power may rest in [him]." Though Paul requested relief from his "thorn in the flesh", he had received word from God: "...my grace is sufficient for you, for my power is made perfect in weakness." (II Corinthians 12:9)

Let us ask God for insight and understanding as we acknowledge our weaknesses.

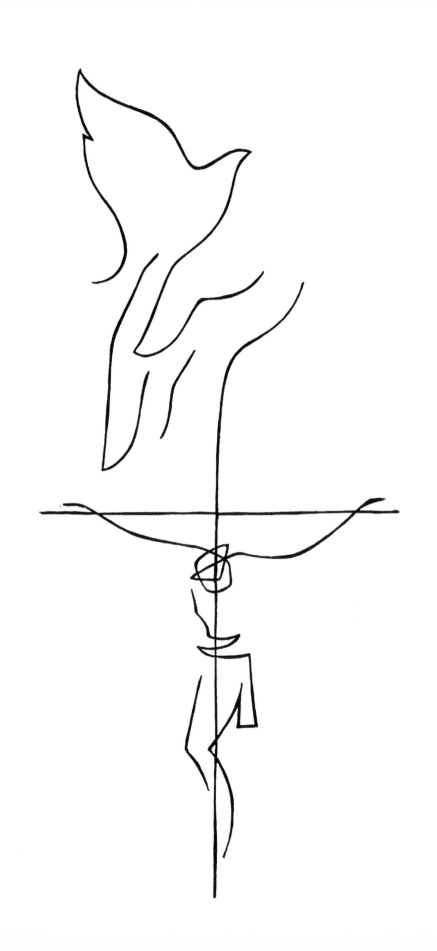

# The Defining Characteristic

"Do you look alike?" This question used to irritate me as a young boy with a twin sister. People's curiosity was sincere, but as a boy, it was annoying that people might think I looked like a girl. However, as I have grown older, I have realized that my sister and I, indeed, share many family physical characteristics. Actually we share more than physical traits, both having a deep love for God, an earnest pursuit of education and a German work ethic. Negative characteristics will remain family secrets! Now as I have children of my own, I realize, more than ever, that the characteristics we pass along are more than physical – some genetic and some the result of nurture, all defining who we are as a family.

Similarly there are characteristics that define the different faiths of the world. In an article entitled, "The Other Jesus," in the March 27, 2000 issue of *Newsweek*, Kenneth L. Woodward elaborated on what different faiths share in common about Jesus. Woodward concluded that all faiths do not view Jesus the same. He explains,

> "Clearly, the cross is what separates the Christ of Christianity from every other Jesus. In Judaism there is no precedent for a Messiah who dies,much less as a criminal as Jesus did. In Islam, the story of Jesus' death is rejected as an affront to Allah himself. Hindus can accept only a Jesus who passes into peaceful samadhi, a yogi who escapes the degradation of death. 'The figure of the crucified Christ,' says Buddhist Thich Nhat Hanh, 'is a very painful image to me. It does not contain joy or peace, and this does not do justice to Jesus.' There is, in short, no room in other religions for a Christ who experiences the full burden of mortal existence-and hence there is no reason to believe in him as the divine Son whom the Father resurrects from the dead."

The cross is the defining characteristic of our faith as followers of Jesus. If Jesus did not die for our sins, then the resurrection was not necessary and our faith is in vain. The apostle Paul articulated this well when he wrote to the church at Corinth, "And if Christ has not been raised, our preaching is useless and so is your faith." (I Corinthians 15:14)

Let us remember with deep gratitude the purchase-price of our adoption into the family of God – the shed blood of Jesus Christ.

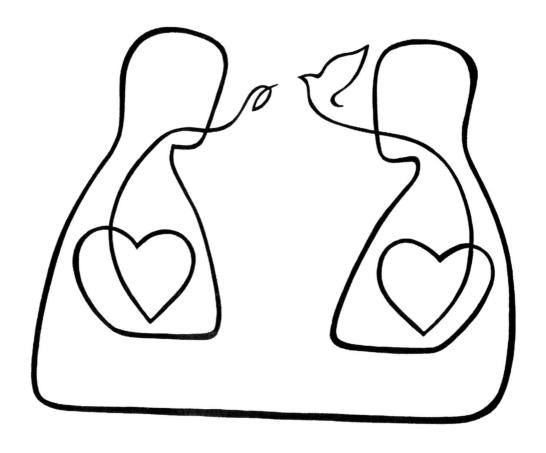

# ⇥ 17 ⇤

## *Words*

The words spoken left me feeling hurt. As I was moping, the advice of a friend echoed in my mind: "Try never to feel hurt from what is said or done to you. Half of the people never intended to hurt you. The other half did, finding great pleasure in your reaction."

This advice, although not entirely true, has seeds of truth in it. Words do impact us; they can hurt or heal. From an early age, when hurt, we are taught to respond with rhymes, such as: "Sticks and stones may break my bones, but words will never hurt me!" Though it is a great rhyme, it is not true. Words are powerful.

A medical colleague once said, "The words we speak can be more powerful than the medicine we give intravenously." The writer of the Proverbs agrees, "Reckless words pierce like a sword, but the tongue of the wise brings healing." (Proverbs 12:18)

The apostle, James, writes "Likewise the tongue is a small part of the body, but it makes great boasts. Consider what a great forest is set on fire by a small spark. The tongue also is a fire, a world of evil among the parts of the body. It corrupts the whole person, sets the whole course of his life on fire, and is itself set on fire by hell. All kinds of animals, birds, reptiles and creatures of the sea are being tamed and have been tamed by man, but no man can tame the tongue. It is a restless evil, full of deadly poison. With the tongue we praise our Lord and Father, and with it we curse men, who have been made in God's likeness. Out of the same mouth come praise and cursing. My brothers, this should not be." (James 3:5-10)

Do our words heal, encourage and minister?

# *Invisibility*

While riding on a tram in Budapest with my wife and a friend, I was reminded of the difficulty of concealing our identities as Americans. We looked like Americans and we spoke to one another in "American English." Our demeanor, our clothes, and our language skills could not help but give us away. We were clearly conspicuous.

Security issues have caused us to assess our ability to be invisible. Blending into a culture has taken on new meaning and importance to us. The principle of "invisibility" has benefits, both personally and professionally.

The organization, for which I work, International Health Services, places a high value on invisibility. We have found that as a foreign organization, enabling and empowering nationals is best done behind the scenes. This requires vigilance in answering the question, "Who gets the credit?"

Invisibility requires that we forfeit our right to credit and recognition, seeking to lift up another rather than to draw attention to ourselves. Jesus modeled this trait, coming to earth to reveal the Father. It was Jesus, "who, being in very nature God, did not consider equality with God something to be grasped, but made himself nothing, taking the very nature of a servant." (Philippians 2:6-7) His purpose was to reveal the nature of His Father, not to seek His own fame. He became "invisible" so that the Father could be "visible."

In András Simon's illustration of Mark 2:1–12 on the previous page, he beautifully depicts four men lowering their paralytic friend through the roof to Jesus, since the house was too crowded to bring him in through the door. The friends are drawn faceless, symbolizing the importance of remaining invisible so that people will see only Jesus.

May we, similarly, seek to remain invisible so that people will see only Jesus in us.

# 19

# Watch Out! Be on your Guard.

As I examine my heart, I am amazed at what I find. It certainly is not all good. One troubling characteristic is greed – wanting more than my share.  It is a disease known to us all, raising its ugly head in our personal lives and our society. We are all too familiar with the collapse of a variety of major businesses due, not only to unfortunate market circumstances, but also to the greed and deception of individuals in leadership. In the 1990's when the stock market and the economy seemed to be on the side of many investors, a *Business Week* magazine cover asked, "Is Greed Good?"

Many in our society would shrug and say, "Maybe." The tide of material pursuit is strong, and in the midst of possessing, we can become possessed with the pursuit.

Jesus warns, "Watch out! Be on your guard against all kinds of greed; a man's life does not consist in the abundance of his possessions." (Luke 12:15)

When the concept of sacrifice (the opposite of greed) is suggested, many hesitate. Os Guiness, in his book, *Steering through Chaos, Vice and Virtue in an Age of Moral Confusion,* suggests that, instead of greed, we as Christ's followers should be known for mercy.  Why contrast mercy with greed?  Mercy is characterized by lavishly seeking more for others through personal sacrifice whereas greed seeks less than justice for others.

Interestingly, greed makes us believe that we deserve more, whereas mercy is blatantly generous, proactively seeking to reach out and give, bringing us to a point where we need less. Patterning our lives after Jesus, produces a generosity of love and material possessions – sometimes requiring the sacrifice of life itself.

Can we begin living extravagantly in mercy, rather than greed?

# 20

# Life is Seldom as it Appears

When I asked an elderly oilman, "What is one of the best lessons you have ever learned in life?" He smiled, replying, "Life is seldom as it seems." Looking beyond the initial impression, comment or situation was, to him, imperative. Only when delving deeper, could he find the truth of the issue at hand.

Often in the emergency department, I have found initial impressions to be deceiving. Trauma due to auto accidents often masks the real issue of a heart attack, stroke, alcoholism or drug addiction. Domestic abuse was often the cause of "incidental injuries." Without peeling back the layers, investigating thoroughly and listening carefully, one could easily be led astray about a patient's fundamental problem.

Spiritually, we are often faced with the same dilemma. Life is seldom as it appears. Jesus, however, is a master at seeing beyond the surface to the heart of people and their issues. For instance, He had an encounter with a Samaritan woman, recorded in the Gospel of John. At first glance, many saw this woman as a worthless human being, not worthy of attention due to sins of her past. To Jesus' disciples, this woman represented someone not even worthy of conversation because of her ethnicity. Yet Jesus recognized that life is seldom as it appears. He looked into her heart and saw great spiritual need and longing. Because He looked more deeply, He was able to meet her needs and satisfy her deepest longings.

Life is seldom as it appears. Let us follow Jesus by looking beyond our initial impressions. "Stop judging by mere appearances, and make a right judgment." (John 7:24)

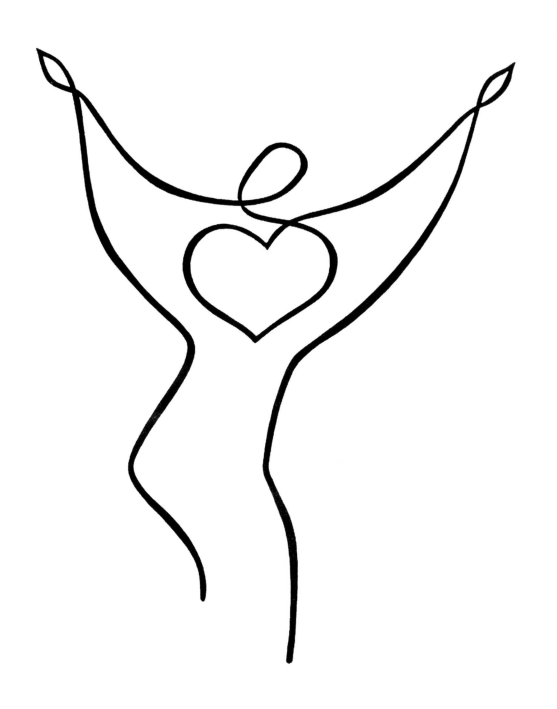

# 21

# *Living with Gratitude*

The crash of our Boeing 767 Hungarian airplane seemed imminent. After climbing to 2000 feet, the plane began losing altitude. Adults and children prepared themselves for a crash. We approached a village just outside Budapest that I knew had a grass airstrip. A crash-landing at this tiny airport seemed certain.

However, as we crossed the airstrip at 500 feet, I was amazed to see the faces of many people waving and cheering. Next, the plane gained altitude, and I guessed that we would try to make it back to the Budapest international airport. Everyone on the plane was anxious and confused since no announcements of any kind had been made. The silence on the plane was heavy.

However, instead of returning to Budapest, the plane climbed to 30,000 feet and made an uneventful trip to New York City. I later learned that our commercial flight had made a "fly-through" at an air show being held at that small airport. Knowing that the danger had passed, I was truly grateful to be alive. But my gratitude was short lived.

While practicing medicine, I had the opportunity to see many people whose lives were saved in the midst of grave medical difficulties. Some responded with gratitude, but others with indifference. Gratitude is often quickly lost when we return to the assurances and routines of life.

However, some never forget the experience of "looking death in the eye." Fyodor Dostoevsky received an unexpected reprieve from his scheduled execution by a firing squad in 1949. The rest of his life was changed with a grateful attitude of a man returned from the dead. Aleksander Solzhenitsyn was miraculously cured of cancer after being discharged from the prison hospital to die. The rest of his life was lived with a renewed purpose, energized by his gratitude.

The apostle Paul tells us, "For the wages of sin is death, but the gift of God is eternal life in Christ Jesus our Lord." (Romans 6:23) Shouldn't we be filled with overwhelming gratitude? Those of us who have been rescued from eternal death have the opportunity to live with reckless abandonment in our spiritual lives.

Let us examine the gratitude in our own hearts. Do we realize how close the brush with death has been?

# 22

# Practice, Practice, Practice

What a magnificent drive off the 16th tee! My golf ball had landed within 10 feet of two other balls that had been equally great drives. As we walked up the fairway I began to congratulate my friends and relive the great shots each of us had made. Our euphoria was broken by the quiet words of one in our group, "It's not over. The real test will be who makes the next shot and the next." The reality of his words echoed in my ears as I sliced my next shot out of bounds into the rough. Consistency is an essential ingredient in both golf and life.

The golf shots of professionals in the last round of a tournament are not random events. They are the product of many lonely hours of practice and the influence of a good coach. Although I may entertain thoughts of skill, any of my great golf shots are random events. Consistent patterns are a result of persistent practice.

As followers of Jesus, our patterns of behavior can only be consistently lived out when we employ *the discipline of practice.* Bearing consistent fruit of "...love, joy, peace, patience, kindness, goodness, faithfulness, gentleness and self-control" (Galatians 5:22) does not happen by chance.

King David recognized this when he said, "This has been my *practice:* I obey your precepts." (Psalm 119:56) Spiritual consistency – a heart and life compatible with our beliefs comes only with practice.

Let us commit to examining our hearts and practicing those behaviors that please God. Maybe I should commit to more practice in golf as well!

# 23

## Being a Material Witness

During my days as a practicing physician, I had many opportunities to go to court. Two of the scenarios that brought me into the legal system were:

- as a material witness in a medical case which I observed, and
- as an expert witness in a medical case for which my opinion was solicited.

As a material witness, I was asked to give an account of what had happened – what I had seen and heard, such as assault, rape or other abusive actions. My credentials as a physician were not an issue; only the truthful expression of what I observed was necessary. As a material witness, there was never anyone testifying against me.

Serving as an expert witness, was an entirely different matter. Both the prosecution and the defense examined my credentials and had to agree that I was an expert. Then I gave a professional opinion about the medical care given in a case in which I had not been involved. As soon as I finished my testimony, another physician would render his opinion concerning the medical care, often presenting a contradictory testimony. Truth, at times, did not seem to be the issue, but rather, who could be the most convincing.

Being a witness is an activity not only in the courtroom. Jesus calls us to be witnesses. When Jesus saw His disciples after the resurrection, he told them, "…and you will be my witnesses in Jerusalem, and in all Judea and Samaria, and to the ends of the earth." (Acts 1:8) I have wondered, in the past, exactly what Jesus meant by "witnesses." Sitting in court one day, I realized that I often try to be an expert witness for Jesus while God is usually asking me to be a material witness. I try to convince people about faith in Jesus (an expert witness' approach). God, however, usually wants me to recount what He has done in my life, which no one can refute (a material witness' approach).

Certainly, God wants some of us to give expert witness concerning Him. But for most of us, our primary responsibility is as a material witness. We see this demonstrated in the life of a demon-possessed man whom Jesus healed (Mark 5:1-20). After being healed, the man begged to go with Jesus, but Jesus said to him, "Go home to your family and tell them how much the Lord has done for you, and how he has had mercy on you." Jesus instructed this man, whose life He had changed, to be a material witness for Him.

Let us also strive to be material witnesses. We have much to tell of what God has done!

# 24

## *The Priority of Love*

Y ou may know this scene, all too well. There are moments when someone in the family is not ready, and it is time to be leaving for church. With one eye fixed on my wristwatch and my impatience clearly communicated, tension begins to fill the air. Unhappiness reigns! On one such Sunday, a disquieting thought entered my mind. "Bob, would you rather be loving or on-time?" Immediately, my reaction was that I would prefer to be both – loving *and* punctual. But since both were not an option, I realized that, on this occasion, I would rather be punctual than loving. What a sad commentary – that I would value an issue of five or ten minutes more than love.

Loving was Jesus' first priority, and He expected the same of His disciples. An expert in the law asked Jesus which was the greatest commandment. Jesus replied that all the law could be summarized in the word *love* – loving God and loving our neighbors. (Matthew 22:34 – 39)

We, like the disciples, find ourselves sidetracked from our priority of love. The worries of the day, personal frustrations, aggravating circumstances and personal agendas distract us from our high calling. Let us honestly examine ourselves, identifying where compromises exist and choose to love.

"A new command I give you: Love one another. As I have loved you, so you must love one another. All men will know that you are my disciples, if you love one another." (John 13: 34–35)

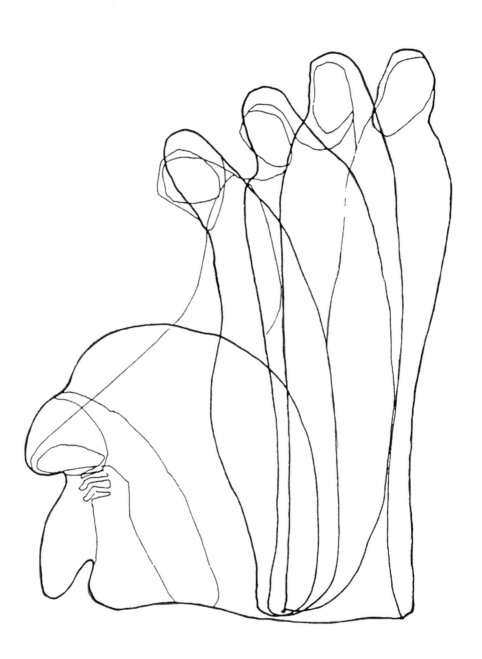

# 25

# Broken People

In the emergency department I have witnessed people physically broken in almost every conceivable way. I have looked at the mangled limbs of young people brought by ambulance or helicopter and thought, "they will never be the same again." In the midst of broken bodies, I have also witnessed broken emotions – hearts broken as loved ones were lost and friends permanently injured. At times, the emergency department can be shrouded in brokenness.

While living in Eastern Europe, I have also witnessed the broken spirits of people displaced from their homelands by war and persecution – refugees struggling daily with dashed hopes and dreams. The heavy burden of these trials drags many to the depths of despair.

God grieves along with us in our suffering. However, He can redeem it for His purposes. Only when we are broken can we yield ourselves to God for transformation. When transformation occurs, peace results. How is that possible? A choice is made to grasp hold of God's grace. A dear friend shared with me the following "equations."

Broken people / under grace → Humility → Peace

Broken people / without grace → Anger, Pride → Bitterness

God is near to broken people. "The Lord is close to the brokenhearted and saves those who are crushed in spirit." (Psalm 34:18) "The sacrifices of God are a broken spirit; a broken and contrite heart, O God, you will not despise." (Psalm 51:17)

We all are broken! We all are wounded! Let us make the choice to grasp hold of the grace of God and allow the Great Physician to lead us to a place of rest that only He can provide.

"Come to me, all you who are weary and burdened, and I will give you rest. Take my yoke upon you and learn from me, for I am gentle and humble in heart, and you will find rest for your souls. For my yoke is easy and my burden is light." (Matthew 11:28-30)

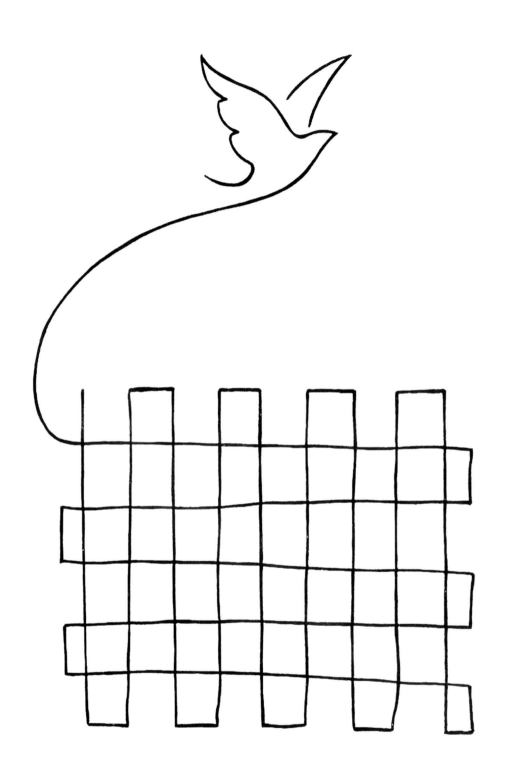

# 26

# Pleasant Places

A letter from friends was filled with good news. Their young family was growing; a summer of rest had invigorated them; and a recent job change had placed them nearer extended family. It appeared that they were in one of those "best of times" periods. Their letter ended with a quote from Psalm 16:6, "The boundary lines have fallen for me in pleasant places; surely I have a delightful inheritance." As a result of this letter, I shared Psalm 16 with my family during a vacation. Being located in a lovely environment made discussing "pleasant places" easy.

However, an MRI done on our daughter several days later quickly changed our perspective as she was diagnosed with a serious medical problem. Our lives suddenly plummeted like a roller coaster from the joys of pleasant walks to the anxiety and despair of difficult medical decisions. We moved from the serenity of unhurried rest to the rapid pace of desperation. The realities of life and death were staring us head-on, and we found ourselves in one of those "worst of times" periods. Where had the pleasant places of Psalm 16 gone?

As our family reread Psalm 16, however, we realized that experiencing the joy and peace of God is not dependent on the circumstances of life. Rather, it is a product of dwelling in the presence of God. Psalm 16:11 says, "You have made known to me the path of life; *you will fill me with joy in your presence*, with eternal pleasures at your right hand." In the midst of our difficulties, we saw repeated evidences of God's presence with us and experienced first hand how God's peace can permeate even life's most grave situations.

Following our daughter's successful brain surgery, we returned to the normal rhythms of life. We will not forget that God provided "pleasant places" in the midst of crisis. These *pleasant places* have nothing to do with physical health, financial security or our feelings. Eternal pleasure is in the presence of God!

# 27

# Unity

March 15th is Hungary's Independence Day. On this date in 1848, Hungary declared its independence from Austria. On that holiday, a Hungarian woman in our church shared a different interpretation of the significance of the day.

She said that March 15th was really a celebration of unity. Over 1,100 years ago, seven nomadic tribes occupied what is now known as Hungary. In order to create a nation, they put away their differences and united under the Magyar tribe, whose leader was Arpad. St. Steven, a descendant of Arpad, was crowned the first king of Hungary. In 1848, a similar event occurred. The Hungarian people put away their many differences and joined to declare independence.

As the woman in church continued, she carefully recounted the difficulties and struggles of the Hungarian people as they fought the Austrian empire, united in the dream for independence. In the end, the Hungarians lost their struggle, but even today, they celebrate Independence Day. She indicated her desire for the Hungarian nation to once again put away their differences and unite. Her prayer is that they will unite under the name of Jesus Christ.

As this delightfully insightful Hungarian woman sat down, I was moved and convicted. This same desire for unity is Jesus' passion, as well. He interceded on our behalf, saying, "I pray also for those who will believe in me through their message, that all of them may be one, Father, just as you are in me and I am in you." (John 17: 20b–21a)

Do we seek to cultivate the unity in the Church for which Christ yearned? What do we allow to separate us? Whatever the issue may be, it keeps us weak and divided. As a result, we are unable to accomplish the tasks that God has given us.

"Therefore, as God's chosen people, holy and dearly loved, clothe yourselves with compassion, kindness, humility, gentleness and patience. Bear with each other and forgive whatever grievances you may have against one another. Forgive as the Lord forgave you. And over all these virtues put on love, which binds them all together in perfect unity." (Colossians 3:12–14)

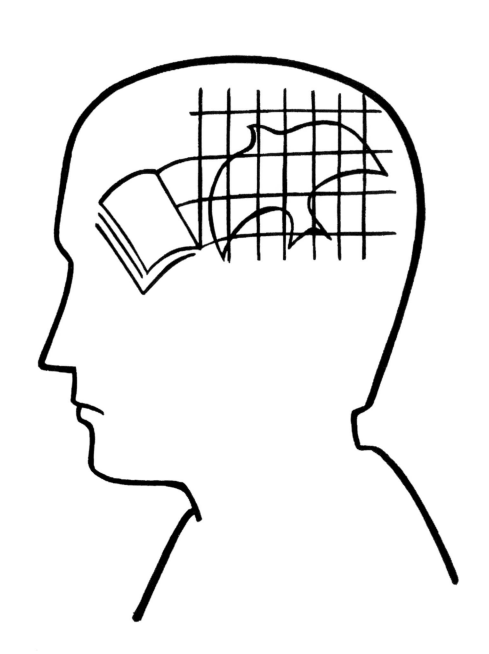

# 28

# The Power of Intent

My *intent* was to lose some excess weight. Intent – does it ring hollow? This word has become weak and diluted in today's language. The dictionary definition is: "to be very attentive, having eyes or thoughts earnestly fixed on something." True intention implies a purpose, design or plan, *not* a casual desire.

The idea of intent has found resonance in the business world. The Harvard Business Review has published articles over the last several decades by scholars such as Michael Porter, Gary Harmel and CK Prahalad, who have developed the concept of "strategic intent." This idea suggests that an organization is better driven by a vision, goals and plans, rather than by analysis of resources and capabilities. When motivated by strategic intent, employees often achieve far more than their capabilities or resources would predict.

The application of "intent" transfers to our lives as followers of Jesus. William Law, in his classic 18th century book, *A Serious Call to A Devout and Holy Life,* wonders, "…why the lives of even avowed Christians are strangely contrary to the principles of Christianity." His answer suggests that a lack of intention may be a key factor. Law states, "Men have not so much intention to please God in all their actions… It is for lack of this intention that you see men who profess religion living in swearing and sensuality."

Without intent, our lives are often lived in casual acceptance of what is allowable, rather than what is commendable. Let us seek to please God with earnest intention. The results of doing so will surely exceed our present resources and capabilities. God blesses our intentions with the power and ability to follow through.

"…for it is God who works in you to will and to act according to his good purpose." (Philippians 2:13)

# 29

# Where Do I Turn?

Have you ever asked for directions, wondering which way to turn, and received the wrong information? Frustrating! I have learned that directions are only as good as their source.

Maps, directions from the gas attendant and even technical instruments such as global positioning devices, help us navigate. Even with these aids, we can lose our way. Great resources fail when the information is inaccurate.

Directions are important, not only in navigating roads, but also in navigating life's choices. Faulty or inaccurate information will lead us astray in our:

- Choices on a personal level
- Choices at work, and
- Choices in our relationships

So what is our source for spiritual direction? We often turn to good Christian books, radio programs or the church, which can provide excellent guidance. But when we wonder where to turn, the only truly reliable guide is Jesus and His Word. Jesus tells us, "I am the way and the truth and the life. No one comes to the Father except through me." (John 14:6)

When King David needed direction, he turned to God saying, "Search me, O God, and know my heart; test me and know my anxious thoughts. See if there is any offensive way in me, and lead me in the way everlasting." (Psalm 139: 23–24)

This week, as we come to intersections on our journey, let us turn to God and His Word – the only fully reliable source.

# 30

# *The Frailty of Life*

I have often witnessed the last minutes of life for people with severe illnesses or traumatic injuries. Most of us rarely think that today could be our last. Yet, over and over again, we are called to witness the reality of death.

A dear friend of mine was 54 years old and in the prime of his life. To the surprise of all, he collapsed while jogging on a health club treadmill (a daily routine) and died. A friend, hearing of the death, wrote to me, "If I knew that today would be my last, I would probably respond differently to the daily events of life." We are so prone to act as though we are immortal, thinking and acting as if we will live forever.

On September 11, 2001, thousands of people awoke, beginning their daily routines, never realizing that they had only hours to live. The impending doom was never forecast, nor was anyone given time to prepare. Death came unexpectedly. Would we act differently if we knew?

Would our relationship to God change if we believed that our next breath could be our last? In "The Letter on Prayer" from the work, *The Cloud of Unknowing,* an anonymous fourteenth-century British writer says to a disciple, "Let me start by saying that the best thing you can do when you start to pray, however long or short your time of prayer…is to tell yourself, and mean it, that you are going to die at the end of your prayer…just think how impossible it is to tell yourself…that you are certain of living longer than the time your prayer takes." This author recognized that a proper understanding of our mortality could change even the way we pray.

When people in the World Trade Center buildings became aware that life was soon to end, they did not pick up their mobile telephones to close one last business deal. Those who were able called family and friends to express their deep love.

The length of our life is not in our hands. Our responses should reflect that fact.

"There is a time for everything, and a season for every activity under heaven: a time to be born and a time to die…" (Ecclesiastes 3:1–2 )

# 31

# Enough is Enough

$A$fter attending a weekend conference on simplicity, my sister introduced me to the concept of "enough", referring to a sufficient amount of material possessions. Being from a western, consumer-oriented, materialistic background, I was intrigued by this discussion. What is enough?

From an early age, the media and various forms of advertising tell us that bigger is better and that there is always something more that we need. The implication – without a new gadget or a particular brand, restlessness and unhappiness will be our lot. This teaches us an untruth – that satisfaction of the heart, mind and soul come from external solutions.

The "enough concept," however, suggests that "more than enough" distracts us and clutters our lives. The clutter of living in excess can undermine peace and rest of the soul. The concept of "enough" enables us to pay attention to the important elements of our lives. "Enough" may vary for different people, and each person needs to honestly assess what that is in his or her own life.

Obviously, "less than enough" has its own challenges. The anxiety of not being able to provide for adequate nourishment and shelter for our bodies is a stark reality. The desperately poor know this all too well.

Jesus, speaking to his followers, addressed this issue of possessions by saying, "Do not store up for yourselves treasures on earth, where moth and rust destroy, and where thieves break in and steal. But store up for yourselves treasures in heaven, where moth and rust do not destroy, and where thieves do not break in and steal." (Matthew 6: 19–20)

The life of Moses portrays this principle. "He [Moses] regarded disgrace for the sake of Christ as of greater value than the treasures of Egypt, because he was looking ahead to his reward." (Hebrews 11:26)

Just what is enough? What is sufficient?

"...My grace is sufficient for you..." (II Corinthians 12:9)

Enough is enough!

# 32

## Simple Can Be Good

$A$t an annual conference of the Peter F. Drucker Foundation for Nonprofit Management, Peter Drucker answered the following question: What are the three greatest lessons you have learned? His response was enlightening in its simplicity. He said, "I'll give you four [answers]:

- If it has to be explained, it won't work.
- Say please and thank you.
- As a writer, if a sentence doesn't gel, don't re-write, re-think it.
- Never ask *who* is right; start by asking what is right."

Winston Churchill once said, "All great things are simple, and many can be expressed in a single word: freedom; justice; honor; duty; mercy; hope."

Speaking in simple terms often facilitates understanding. This also applies to the way in which we express our faith. When describing our relationship to the eternal God, we commonly use words that confuse. However, many of the great doctrines of the Bible can be explained in monosyllables that little children can understand:

- God loves you.
- Christ died for you.
- Trust in God's Son, Jesus.
- Love God and others.

In a television interview several decades ago, the new moderator of a major denomination in the United States was asked, "What is the most profound truth you have ever heard?" He replied, "Jesus loves me this I know, for the Bible tells me so." How grateful I am that the infinite God of the universe willingly reduced Himself and became man so that we might, with simplicity, understand Him.

Let us consider how we communicate God's truths to family, friends and colleagues. Can our words be simplified?

"For God so loved the world that he gave his one and only Son, that whoever believes in him shall not perish but have eternal life." (John 3:16)

# 33

# The Power of Serving

The nurses stopped their work and stood up as we entered the Intensive Care Unit. "What is going on?" I thought. As a first-year medical student working with an older doctor, I was totally confused. Later when I asked, the doctor indicated, with some smugness, that the nurses stood up to recognize his entrance. He was using his position to demand respect. I have never forgotten that very uncomfortable moment.

It is so easy to fall into patterns of exerting power and control inappropriately, whether at work or at home. As a physician, I gave orders all day. Then I would come home and, at times, automatically continue giving orders- not a good strategy for family life.

The power of position or authority can be exercised for two very different advantages – our own or another's. Whether as parents or as leaders in work or ministry, we all choose how to use power. Unfortunately, we sometimes choose to our own advantage.

Jesus, however, tells us to make this choice for the advantage of others. When two of his disciples requested special positions of power in the Kingdom of God, Jesus said, "You know that the rulers of the Gentiles lord it over them, and their high officials exercise authority over them. Not so with you. Instead, whoever wants to become great among you must be your servant, and whoever wants to be first must be your slave – just as the Son of Man did not come to be served, but to serve, and to give his life as a ransom for many." (Matthew 20:25–28)

When God chose to enter time and space, he did not come as a powerful political leader or as an erudite ecclesiastical head. Rather, the omnipotent and omniscient God came clothed as a babe in a manger. God used His power in the person of Jesus for our eternal advantage.

The position of authority is the prime opportunity for serving. In the arenas where we have influence, power or position, we have a choice - to advocate for and serve ourselves or to advocate for and serve others. Let us follow Jesus' example.

# 34

# Trusting God's Purposes

"How's business?" Having not seen my British friend in some time, I was anxious to catch up on his life. I quickly realized that this was not the best of times for him. His business had taken a significant downturn. This was especially worrisome since his wife was pregnant with their first child. He had hoped financial realities would be different. His parting words touched me deeply as he said, "I am trying to seek the face of God, not His hand! It is much easier to look for the provisions of God, rather than His purpose."

We are so often driven in finding solutions to our problems that we seldom stop to recognize what God might have us learn. C. S. Lewis wrote that pain is God's megaphone through which He speaks to a deaf world.

For seven heartbreaking years, Adoniram Judson, the renowned missionary to Burma (today called Myanmar), endured hunger, deprivation, imprisonment, and torture. As a result, he carried ugly scars made by the chains and iron shackles which had cruelly bound him. Undaunted, upon his release he asked for permission to enter another province where he could resume preaching the gospel. The godless leader indignantly denied his request, saying, "My people are not fools enough to listen to anything a missionary might say, but I fear they might be impressed by your scars and turn to your religion." Although Judson's trials must have seemed purposeless at the time, he undoubtedly looked back, with wonder, at God's ability to redeem the suffering as his scars became a powerful witness to the reality of God.

In the Bible, Joseph, looking back on his life, realized how God used many difficult circumstances, redeeming them for His purposes. When speaking to his brothers, Joseph said, "You intended to harm me, but God intended it for good to accomplish what is now being done, the saving of many lives." (Genesis 50: 20)

Do we trust God enough to rest in the knowledge of His purposes rather than to only seek His deliverance from difficult circumstances?

"For it has been granted to you on behalf of Christ not only to believe on him, but also to suffer for him..." (Philippians 1:29)

# 35

## Security

"I feel more unsettled and insecure than any time in my life." These words by a very successful physician forced me to re-think this issue. Our intense desire for security often causes us to trust in that which leads us away from *ultimate* security. We are told to strategize our vocations and plan financially, both of which are prudent. Even politically, we desire to elect governments that will insure stability. But does vocational, financial and political surety bring lasting security?

Alexis de Tocqueville's *Democracy in America*, written as a two volume treatise in 1835 and 1840, observed how the new American democracy affected society from politics to poetry. Although most of his observations were positive, he noted that the American desire for material well-being often bred anxiety rather than satisfaction. Mr. de Tocqueville wrote, "It is a strange thing to see with what sort of feverish ardor Americans pursue well-being and how they show themselves constantly tormented by a vague fear of not having chosen the shortest route that can lead to it."

Donald Mitchell, the former head of International Quality Assurance for General Motors, gave this definition of insecurity to a group of Hungarian businessmen in Budapest, "Insecurity is building your life on anything that can be taken away from you." Yet most of our efforts toward acquiring security consist of pursuing the temporal and the material.

The Apostle Paul would have agreed with Mr. Mitchell. "Let each carpenter who comes on the job take care to build on the foundation! Remember, there is only one foundation, the one already laid: Jesus Christ. Take particular care in picking out your building materials. Eventually there is going to be an inspection. If you use cheap or inferior materials, you'll be found out." (I Corinthians 3:10b–13a; *The Message*)

On what are we building our hope for security in the future?

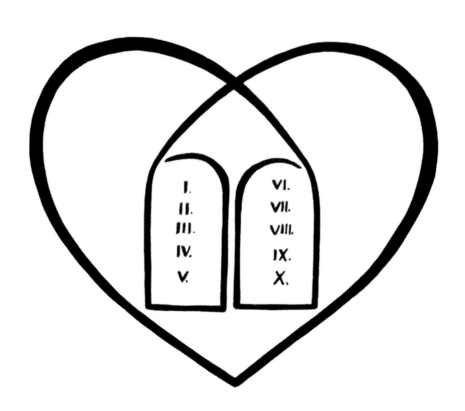

# 36

*Telling Stories*

Storytelling plays an important role in what a culture defines as its values The dangers of losing the important stories of a culture are insightfully chronicled in Allan Bloom's classic book, *The Closing of the American Mind.* He suggests that we have

- Displaced moral truth in our stories with a mixture of destructive values and
- Substituted reason in our stories for the trivial pursuit of relevance.

Part of the strength of the past, says Dr. Bloom, was found in sharing "great stories."

Bloom says, "My grandparents were ignorant people by our standards, and my grandfather held only lowly jobs.  But their home was spiritually rich because all the things done in it, not only what was specifically ritual, found their origin in the Bible's commandments and their explanation in the Bible's stories. . ." Dr. Bloom, a University of Chicago professor, whose spiritual roots are Jewish, suggests these rich traditions have been lost, the stories – forgotten.

Maintaining a culture filled with moral values, community strength and spiritual depth requires work. The sacred stories must be told over and over again especially when society is bombarded by easier, less rich scripts on television and in movies. Moses admonished the children of Israel, reminding them to pass on the narratives of God's faithfulness. He implored them saying, "Impress them on your children. Talk about them when you sit at home and when you walk along the road, when you lie down and when you get up." (Deuteronomy 6:7)

What are the stories our children are learning from us and our home environments?

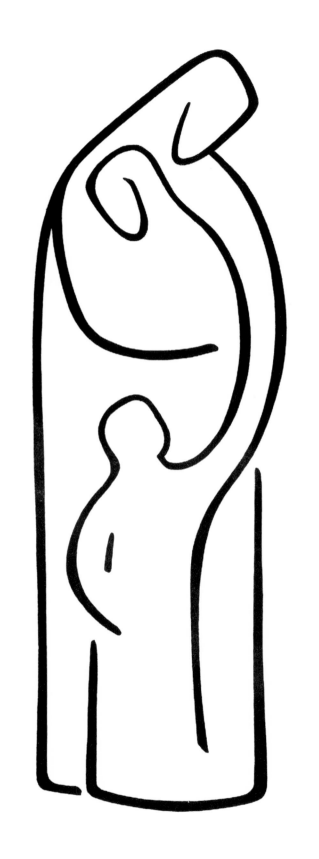

# 37

# Community: A Source of Life

Living in Budapest, Hungary, exposed me to the many contrasts of city life. In the midst of masses of people and much activity, loneliness abounded. I was reminded that community and relationships are vital for well-being.

Some confuse loneliness with solitude. Yet, solitude can be a precious time when one willfully withdraws from interaction in order to be renewed. In the absence of regular and meaningful relationship, however, aloneness can be dangerous. Dietrich Bonhoeffer commented on this difference when he wrote, "Let him who cannot be alone beware of community...But the reverse is also true: let him who is not in community beware of being alone." God never intended that we be alone, out of relationship with others.

The psychiatrist, Dr. Leonard Cammer, articulated the incredible need of the human heart for relationship. He said, "A telephone call to a depressed person can save a life. An occasional word, a ten-minute visit, can be more effective then twenty-four hours of nursing care. You can buy nursing care. You can't buy love."

The description of the early church shows the pattern designed for relationship. "They devoted themselves to the apostles' teaching and to the fellowship, to the breaking of bread and to prayer." (Acts 2:42)

God created people for relationship – with Him and with others. Is there someone we know for whom our relationship is vital and could be an expression of God's love? Let us commit to sharing our love with someone who is lonely.

# 38

# Correct Diagnosis and Treatment

A correct diagnosis is essential when assessing a medical problem. Wouldn't you agree? I have observed people formulating treatment plans in the absence of accurate diagnoses. The consequences can be devastating.

A patient's understanding of his or her disease is also vital for effective treatment. For instance, I remember an elderly man who came into my emergency department. Skin cancer had eaten away his nose and part of his face. Several years prior, he had been told he had skin cancer and that a simple surgical procedure could cure him. But he refused to accept the diagnosis and the treatment. Instead, he chose to use vitamins and alternative medical treatments. The results were catastrophic.

Spiritually, a correct diagnosis is important as well. At times, I, like the elderly man with cancer, cannot comprehend the diagnosis, in this case the total depravity of my soul. As an acceptable member of society – active in church and community, I often lose sight of my spiritual diagnosis – *sinner*. Underestimating the seriousness of the diagnosis, makes me think that the treatment is simple. I try sinning a little less and try doing a little more service for God. Failing to accept the diagnosis or its gravity, allows me to think that I can solve the problem myself.

When considering our spiritual condition, the diagnosis is sin. The treatment provided by God is Jesus' blood. The spiritual outcome is forgiveness and grateful service to God. We must never minimize the gravity of our spiritual condition nor minimize the redeeming power of the treatment.

"In him we have redemption through his blood, the forgiveness of sins, in accordance with the riches of God's grace" (Ephesians 1:7)

# 39

## *Listening*

"After listening to your story, examining you and reviewing your electro-cardiogram and blood tests, I believe that you have a pulled muscle in your chest. That is my impression, but how do my thoughts fit with your opinion?" My 25-year-old emergency department patient began to cry. He told me of his terrible fear that he was having a heart attack. His father had recently died of a heart attack and he was fearful that the same was happening to him. I was grateful to have the opportunity to assuage those fears. Earlier in my medical career, I would not have been as sensitive to ask or hear the thoughts of a patient. My orientation was "find the problem and fix it." What a mistake.

Perhaps listening and learning from others is not an issue for you. However, with me, I find this problem cropping up everywhere in my life. For instance, when my wife Pamela is talking, I am often not listening, but formulating my response. A friend of mine has always encouraged me to be a good student of my wife – a noble subject for study. Needless to say, I am often insensitive and miss the point because I do not listen and learn. My children, my colleagues and my patients have also experienced the frustration of times when I do not listen. The question I answer is sometimes not the one that is asked, or the comment I acknowledge has more to it than I hear.

At times, my relationship with God is like that as well. I am fixated on the issues for which I want God's intervention and miss listening and learning from Him. When Jesus was on earth, He spent much of His time teaching the disciples. He answered their questions and taught them from life situations and through parables, giving them instructions on how to live. Just as He did with the disciples, Jesus desires to do that with you and me. He has given us His Word and His Spirit to guide us into a fuller understanding of the truth. If only we would stop and listen.

"My sheep listen to my voice; I know them, and they follow me." (John 10:27)

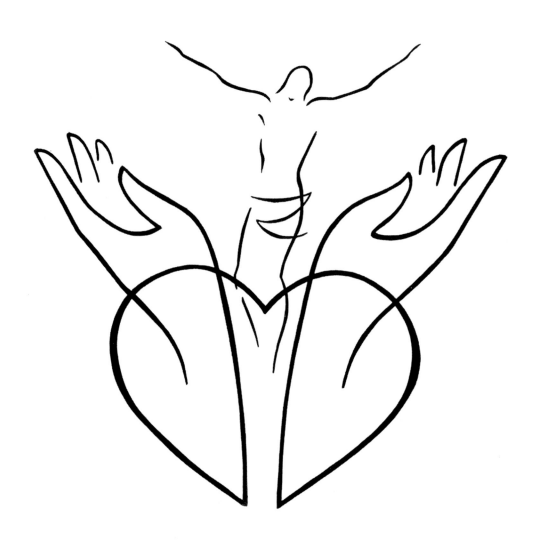

# 40

# Treasure or Junk?

Have you ever confused a piece of junk for a treasure? I remember the first time this problem of discernment occurred for me. I was a young boy at a farm auction. I saw what I thought was a beautiful antique peck/half-peck bucket. I was excited to bid on this object of my desire and succeeded. But as my treasure was being passed back to me, my joy turned to despair as the bucket completely fell apart. My first experience with judging between treasures and junk was a failure.

People all over the world visit flea markets, yard sales and special stores designed to make money from unwanted material goods. The joy comes in finding treasures in the midst of junk. Much energy is often consumed in the search, but the sense of satisfaction is sweet when a treasure is found.

Spiritually the same challenge exists. We often confuse junk for treasure. Referring to the treasure of "the knowledge of the glory of God in the face of Christ," Paul says, "But we have this treasure in jars of clay to show that this all-surpassing power is from God and not from us." (II Corinthians 4:7)

At times, it is easy to confuse what is the treasure and what is the jar of clay. We might believe that we are the treasure in our love and service for God. At other times, we might think that our church or special group is the treasure. The truth is that "the knowledge of the glory of God in the face of Christ", is the treasure. We are the jars of clay.

What a treasure!

# 41

# Topics of Conversation

I cannot count how many hospital and medical staff dinners my wife Pamela and I have attended. Often following these occasions, Pamela would comment that too much of the conversations centered on medical talk. When businessmen or sports fanatics gather together, the same phenomenon easily occurs. Talk quickly gravitates towards shared interests. It is unavoidable. Put people together who have a common passion and conversation will quickly steer in that direction.

Yet when followers of Christ get together, what is the focus of discussion? I am afraid that conversations about our passion for Christ are not as common as I wish. However, I have one friend who always engages me in five questions to measure my passions. They are:

- How are you loving God?
- How are you loving Pamela?
- How are you loving your daughters?
- How are you loving your colleagues?
- How are you loving friends?

This friend always focuses his questions on the two great commands of Jesus – to love God with all our heart, mind, soul and strength and to love our neighbor as ourselves. Although, there have been times when I dreaded answering his questions, I appreciate how he helped keep my priorities in the right places.

What is the focus of discussion when we converse with friends and followers of Christ? Is it politics, medicine, sports or family? There is nothing inherently wrong with those topics. But, do we also joyfully recount the goodness and mercy of the Lord? If a stranger walked into our midst, would he or she easily identify our passion for Christ?

"May the words of my mouth and the meditations of my heart be pleasing in your sight, O Lord, my Rock and my Redeemer. (Psalm 19:14)

# 42

# A Sweet Aroma

Smell – how infrequently I am consciously grateful for this sense. A recent trip to the farming area of Lancaster County, Pennsylvania, the home of many of my relatives, brought back memories galore – all the result of aromas and fragrances. I was so grateful for the sense of smell. The rich aroma of freshly baked bread and pies brought back memories of visits to my grandparents. The earthy fragrances of barns restored memories of time spent on the farms of my uncles and aunts. Wonderfully full and distinct pictures were resurrected through the power of smell. Some physiologists and neuro-anatomists believe that this may result from the close proximity of the olfactory (smell) area of the brain and the hippocampus, where it is believed that memory resides. Whatever the reason, my mind exploded with memories as a result of smell.

Later that same week I developed a stuffy nose. It was hard to tell whether this was the result of a cold or allergies, but the outcome was the same – discomfort, decreased ability to smell and taste and reduced awareness of my environment. Memories related to smell were impossible in such a condition. As a physician, smell also plays a vital role. Antiseptic aromas greeted me daily as I entered the hospital. Occasionally, encounters with sick patients revealed a specific disease such as an infection with the pseudomonas bacteria that emits an odor never to be forgotten. How valuable is the sense of smell!

All these thoughts about smell cause me to wonder how this sense relates to my spiritual life. Interestingly, the phrase "an aroma pleasing to the Lord" (Exodus 29:18; Numbers 15:3) is an expression used in the Old Testament to affirm God's acceptance of a sacrifice brought to Him. The apostle Paul spoke of Jesus' death on the cross as a "fragrant offering and sacrifice to God." (Ephesians 5:2) Paul also expressed the view that his life and ministry had a fragrance. To some, this aroma attracted, and to others, repulsion was the response.

"But thanks be to God, who always leads us in triumphal procession in Christ and through us spreads everywhere the fragrance of the knowledge of him. For we are to God the aroma of Christ among those who are being saved and those who are perishing." (2 Corinthians 2:14–15)

God created us in His image – with a sense of smell. Let us be a sweet aroma.

# 43

# The Object of Our Faith

"Many say they live by faith, but few actually do." A medical school dean who had been born in Hungary spoke these words to me. Under Communism, her faith had been tested frequently. For instance, her mother turned her over to the authorities because of her interest in God. Her father held a knife over her, trying to cause her to waiver. She was denied entrance into the university because of what she believed. Even a secret police official offered her a favor of acceptance into the university in exchange for denying her faith. Yet she boldly proclaimed her belief in Jesus. Faith was not an abstract concept to her.

Faith is one of those words that we often use in Christian messages. Sometimes we think that faith is something we do to make the unlikely more possible. We often think of it as a subjective effort, as if our spiritual strength was the issue. The Bible, however, links faith to that which is certain and assuredly true. The emphasis is not on our efforts toward faith, but rather the object of our faith – God, Himself.

The lessons of faith from this medical school dean were dramatic, but they reveal simple truths.

- Faith is an assurance in an unseen God, not the product of our efforts.
- Faith transforms us through our personal trust in God through Jesus Christ.
- Faith is revealed in our lives through simple, child-like trust in God.

We are repeatedly commanded, as followers of Jesus, to be people of faith. Let us boldly and confidently express the object of our faith – The Lord Jesus Christ.

"… The life I live in the body, I live by faith in the Son of God, who loved me and gave himself for me." (Galatians 2:20)

# 44

## The Mundane

"Significance", "Impact" and "Doing the Impossible" are some of the slo-gans I hear in the Christian community today. These are certainly noble ambitions. However, what happens when we are called to do the simple, routine and mundane tasks of life? A Christian magazine author bemoaned the fact that mundane chores such as laundry, home repairs, personal finances, sorting mail, preparing food and cleaning bathrooms were preventing her from doing the "important." Do we feel, at times, that the routine tasks of everyday life are keeping us from accomplishing great things for God?

Does faithfulness in the unseen events have just as much importance as the events that are seen? Brother Lawrence's book, *The Practice of the Presence of God*, illustrates the contentment one can experience serving God in the kitchen. Brother Lawrence called himself "the lord of all pots and pans." He found God in the kitchen by turning his chores into "the sacrament of the present moment."

To me, one of the most incredible moments in the life of Jesus was when He prepared breakfast on the shore for his disciples. Following His death and res-urrection, Jesus appeared to them while they were out on the lake fishing. As they steered their boat toward shore, Jesus cooked breakfast. (John 21:11-14) Can you imagine? The God of the Universe knelt in the sand to start a fire and serve his friends. Can we scoff at such tasks if God did not?

The fact is that big projects of life can not transform society in the same way that small ones can. Small tasks keep families functioning, hospitals clean and organizations running. The task does not determine the value of a person's work. As Christians our worth is found in Christ, not in the size or nature of the job.

Oh, that we might be like Brother Lawrence, turning our chores – big or little – into "the sacrament of the moment"!

"Jesus said to them, `Come and have breakfast.'" (John 21:12a)

# 45

## *Gifts Transformed*

On a recent trip to the country of Moldova, I was overwhelmed with the enormity of the needs. Having formerly belonged to the Soviet Union, it is a country presently steeped in poverty and political confusion. My immediate reaction was despair, thinking to myself, "What do I have to offer that will impact this country's incredible needs?" Later, I thought of people in the Bible who had similar thoughts:

- Moses who said, "Who am I? I can not speak."
- Jeremiah who said, "I am only a young man."
- The disciples, when confronting 5,000 hungry men, said, "We have only…"

We deny the power and creativity of God when we think that our limited abilities and resources are not enough for Him to use.

A Sunday school teacher from my childhood days continues to teach me important lessons. She had an opportunity to support a ministry by praying and giving financially. Initially, she was discouraged assessing her present financial commitments which were stretched by her modest pension. She realized, however, that every gift is transformed in the hands of God. So she said, "I will give a little, so God can multiply." Her five dollars a month and fervent prayers are a lavish gift to God.

In God's hands, our gifts are transformed.

- Our hearts are enlarged.
- Our resources are creatively used.
- Our time is reordered.

Do you, like me, feel overwhelmed with the issues of personal life, society and the world? Jesus calls us to follow Him and to bring all that we have, meager though it may appear, for His creative use. Let us do that today.

"He also saw a poor widow put in two very small copper coins. 'I tell you the truth,' he said, 'This poor widow has put in more than all the others. All these people gave their gifts out of their wealth; but she out of her poverty put in all she had to live on.'" (Luke 21:2–4)

# 46

# Giving or Taking

In my medical school days, still unmarried, I was interested in finding a community that included young ladies. My church, at that time, had a Sunday night coffee house. Each week included great music, lots of people and a "one minute message." Some people came to hear the music. Others came to hear the "one minute message." However, I came to meet girls. I never helped with the planning or assisted in the work of the coffee house. You might say I came, not to give, but to get.

Whether we come to give or to get affects the community itself. Henri Nouwen, the Dutch author and theologian, suggests that two different attitudes produce two very different results. He says:

- Those whose hearts are right with God enrich, serve and heal in community.
- Those whose hearts are not right with God take from and destroy community.

We find both of these types of people in our fellowships of faith.

Interestingly, when Jesus entered into community with mankind, he came as a servant, not as a king. He came to give and to provide. His life is the ultimate example of how we should behave in our communities.

How are we doing in the communities where God has placed us? Are we giving or taking?

"Each one should use whatever gift he has received to serve others, faithfully administering God's grace in its various forms." (I Peter 4:10)

# 47

# *Failure*

Failure is not a pleasant subject for study. This is especially true in our high self-esteem-conscious society. To some it is a terrible curse that is to be avoided at all costs – or is it? An Arabic proverb says, "Endless sunshine gives birth to a desert."

A friend living in Latvia, shared with me three concepts he has learned in moments of defeat:

- Failure teaches us lessons we could not otherwise learn. For example, it was during the disciples' failures – such as their inability to catch fish or heal the epileptic – that they were able to hear and learn some of Jesus' greatest lessons.
- Lack of success allows us the opportunity for humility through which God's grace can flow. Failing has a wonderful way of knocking down the pride that hinders us from receiving God's grace.
- Failure enables God to test our faithfulness.

What may appear as failure can truly be success if we learn, change, and adapt as a result. With this perspective, Peter saw trials, of which failure is one, as an opportunity to grow in his faith.

"…for a little while you may have had to suffer grief in all kinds of trials. These have come so that your faith – of greater worth than gold, which perishes even though refined by fire – may be proved genuine and may result in praise, glory and honor when Jesus Christ is revealed." (I Peter 1:6b-7)

Let us join Peter, viewing our failures as opportunity.

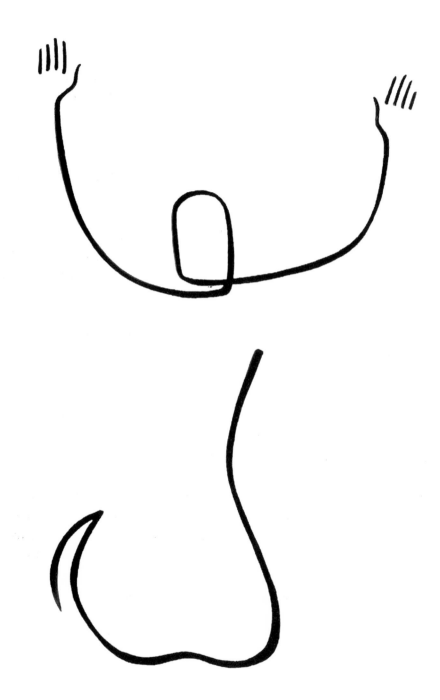

# 48

## *Brilliance*

The very first day of medical school is etched in my memory. Sitting in front of me, a fellow classmate was reading *Les Misérables*. I was struck by his casual attitude compared to my nervous anticipation. Since I had never read *Les Misérables*, I looked more closely and realized that he was reading it in French! Immediately intimidated, I thought this guy had to be brilliant. Over the next four years, however, I came to understand that he was absolutely brilliant in certain areas, but in other arenas of life he was less than stellar.

Recently, a friend used the word "brilliant" repeatedly while describing his boss. But as he elaborated on the life of his boss, he depicted 14-hour workdays, six and seven days a week. He verbally sketched a picture of a man willing to sacrifice his children's baseball games and his wife's birthday for the good of the job. His Ivy League and Oxford education coupled with his clever intellect could not compensate for his disastrous lack of brilliance in his personal life.

Since we all have areas of brilliance and areas of "dullness" in our lives, I began to wonder about my own, specifically with regard to my spiritual life. I want to be known as a "brilliant" follower of Jesus. But what characterizes such a person?

In my dictionary, the first definition of 'brilliant' has nothing to do with "having great ability," but rather, it speaks of possessing a particular trait – that of "shining brightly." I then realized that being a brilliant follower of Jesus has nothing to do with natural abilities, but rather, reflecting the brilliance of Jesus.

The Apostle Paul alludes to this when he says, "And we, who with unveiled faces all reflect the Lord's glory, are being transformed into his likeness with ever-increasing glory, which comes from the Lord, who is the Spirit."
(II Corinthians 3:18)

As followers of Jesus, do we reflect the brilliance of our Master?

# 49

# *Looking Inside*

I will never forget the first time I saw a living, beating heart. This life-giving pump did not look anything like the hearts of Valentine cards. In fact, it bore little resemblance to the static pictures in my anatomy textbook.

I was a third-year medical student working in the cardiac intensive care unit. Suddenly, a patient's heart ruptured. A cardio-thoracic surgeon making his daily rounds quickly accessed the situation. Without hesitation, he opened the patient's chest and exposed the throbbing heart. He then placed a suture through the hole in the heart – quite a dramatic moment. I was assigned the task of holding the life-saving suture as we rushed the patient to the operating room to complete the job of repairing his heart.

As I stared at that pulsating muscle, I was amazed at how my previous conception of the heart differed from its true nature. What we perceive from the outside is often different from the reality of the inside. This is true in our spiritual lives, as well.

The Bible emphasizes that God peers through our external facades to assess the reality of the heart. The Old Testament prophet Jeremiah said, "The heart is deceitful above all things and beyond cure. Who can understand it?" (Jeremiah 17:9) Obviously, Jeremiah was not referring to the human organ that circulates blood. Rather, he was speaking of the spiritual heart of the inner man.

The former president of Hungary, Arpad Goncz, recognized the importance of tending to the heart when he said that Hungary will not move forward until the hearts of its people are changed. So often we focus our efforts on making external changes, tending to the symptoms of evil, rather than to the disease itself. We employ armies, police forces, prisons and new laws. Yet, no lasting change can occur until the human heart is transformed.

God promises to do just that! He has offered to be that agent of transformation – cleansing, mending and healing our hearts.

May our hearts' prayer be, as the Psalmist declared, "Create in me a pure heart, O God, and renew a steadfast spirit within me." (Psalm 51:10)

# 50

# *Where is Home?*

Knowledge of one's destination is an essential component of any journey. Can you imagine intending to drive home, having no idea where home is?

This question – "Where is home?" – is not as easy to answer as it might first appear. As ex-patriots living in Hungary, the answer often seemed elusive. How do we define home? Is it a house? A town? Our family? Our emotional or cultural attachments? For us, the answers lie in both the United States and Hungary. Our hearts are pulled in two directions.

The "tug-of-war" between our earthly home and our spiritual home is similar. We find ourselves becoming attached to the things of this earth. As the Lord calls us in one direction, the world tugs us in another. Our hearts easily become confused, and peace eludes us.

The apostle Paul, in his letter to the Philippians, reminds us of the true location of our home, saying, "But our citizenship is in heaven." (Philippians 3:20a) His message to the Corinthians further explains this concept.

"Compared to what's coming, living conditions around here seem like a stopover in an unfurnished shack, and we're tired of it! We have been given a glimpse of the real thing, our true home, our resurrection bodies! The Spirit of God whets our appetite by giving us a taste of what's ahead. He puts a little of heaven in our hearts so that we'll never settle for less." (II Corinthians 5:2–5; *The Message*)

Are we too comfortable here in our earthly home, forgetting that this is merely a temporary residence? Do we long for our spiritual home? Are we homesick to be with our Father?

# About the Illustrator

András Simon, a renowned Hungarian artist, communicates Biblical truth through his unique and beautiful line drawings. Because of his faith, he was rejected twice from Hungary's Art Academy. András, however, was not deterred from developing and utilizing his gifts. In 1984 he offered his talents to God, desiring that his work would cause others to praise the Lord. András' prayer has been answered as his drawings have touched the hearts of people in numerous countries around the world. Many private collections contain his prints, including the home the former Hungarian president, Árpád Göncz and the Vatican.

His talents do not end with his easel. Most of you have yet to experience the delight of hearing András play his shepherd's flute. His tunes lift the listener to "higher ground". András is also a writer of meditations. His quiet and thoughtful spirit is a joy to many. He lives in Budapest, Hungary with his wife and four children.

# About the Author

Bob Snyder spent 20 years practicing medicine — many of those years as co-chairman of the Emergency Medicine department at Brandywine hospital, Coatesville, Pennsylvania. He continues as an affiliate faculty member in the Department of Emergency Medicine of Thomas Jefferson University.

Bob was very content in his work in emergency medicine, when God called him and his family to ministry in Hungary (1996). As a result, International Health Services (IHS) was born. IHS trains and mentors Christian medical professionals, teaching them how to integrate their faith in Jesus into their medical practices, ultimately impacting patients' lives, their families and their communities. The Snyder's returned to the U.S. in 2003 to continue the work of IHS.

For Bob, life has become a journey. As the years go by, he now sees lessons to be learned, some of them painful, some constant reminders, and most life-long truths. He is the proud father of three daughters, and a life-partner in ministry with his wife. He works at golf, enjoys a good baseball game, and will never understand why his wife does not appreciate football. His greatest love is . . . Jesus.